# Hey Big Boy!

## A Message to a Son

ISBN - 13: 978-0615565552
ISBN - 10: 0615565557
Windsor, CT
Printed in the United States of America

For Miles...my little Prince!
You are the inspiration and motivation for
this work.  Thanks for being my Big Boy!
-Love Dad


For all young men...you are a precious gift, and
the future generation of greatness.  I am confident
in your ability to do the extraordinary.  Believe
that you can!


For all parents who are blessed with the awesome
responsibility of raising a son...May this book spark
questions from your child, and generate conversations
that deepen your relationship.

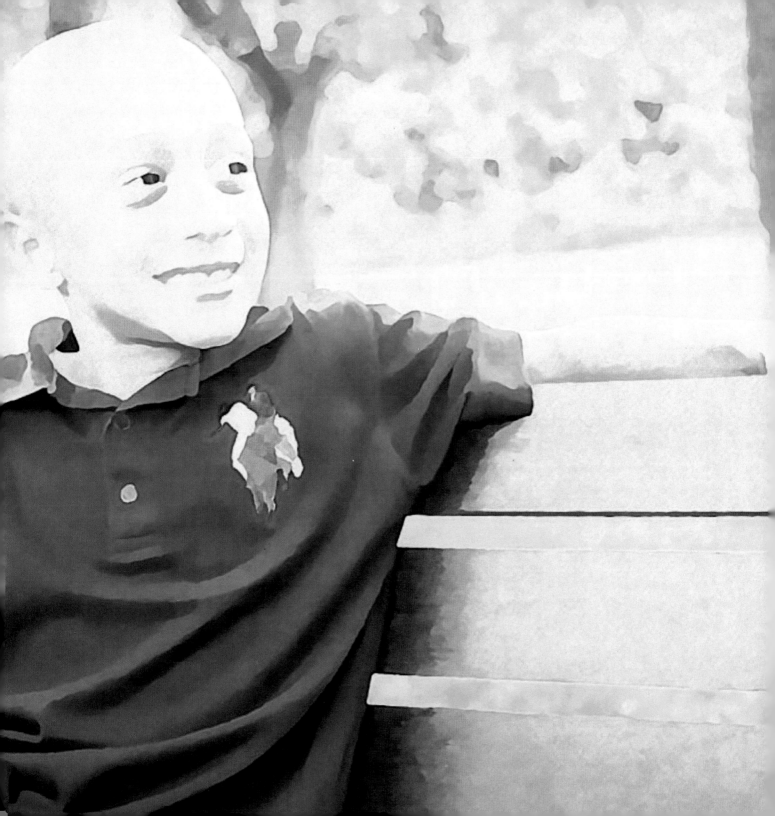

Hey Big Boy,

with your wide beaming smile,

sit down beside me,

and let's talk awhile.

I cannot believe

that you are growing so fast,

it is hard to believe

all the time that has passed.

Over the years,

I have witnessed it all,

each bump, each bruise,

each stumble, each fall.

Each major milestone

your sadness, your joy.

all that has made you,

an incredible boy.

Hey Big Boy,

   learn all you can,

Knowledge is power,

   in life's crazy plan.

Education is a key,

   that opens many doors.

seize every moment,

   strive to obtain more.

Life is filled with ups and downs,

   always get up, whenever you fall.

Dust yourself off,

      have faith and believe,

regain your focus,

      strive to achieve!.

Hey Big Boy,

　　　　what's on your mind?

When you need to talk,

　　I'll be here every time.

I promise I'll listen,

　　any time of day,

whether good or bad,

　　let's hear what you have to say.

You will grow up

To be a big strong man.

I will prepare you

the best that I can.

Learn from my mistakes,

as you encounter your own.

Apply the lessons you learn

along life's winding road.

Hey Big Boy,

    with your big bright eyes,

they sparkle like glitter,

      and the stars in the sky.

When you look at me

    with the trust that you do,

I will do any thing in the world

    that I need to for you.

Ask and it shall be given,

seek and you will find.

I'll set the example,

for you to follow behind.

I will share words of wisdom,

as we walk side by side.

Remember that your steps "are ordered,"

so let the Lord be your guide.

Know your strengths from your struggles,

and understand each.

Don't lose your strength to your struggles,

if you want to succeed.

Treat people with respect,

fairness, and dignity too.

Never accept less,

when people deal with you.

Hey Big Boy,

with your outstretched hands.

When they reach out to grab me,

you must understand.

Whenever you need me,

I will be there.

So feel free to reach,

any time, any where.

Always remember

to hold your head up high.

The world is yours to conquer,

just be willing to try.

Believe in yourself,

like all winners do.

Speak life into your dreams,

and watch them come true!

Hey Big Boy,

you are a reflection of me.

You are an image of God,

a child of destiny

If ever you should wonder,

I want you to know,

you're my little Prince,

And I love you so.